Pebble®

Families

Fathers

Revised and Updated

by Lola M. Schaefer

Consulting Editor: Gail Saunders-Smith, PhD

Capstone
press®

Mankato, Minnesota

Pebble Books are published by Capstone Press,
151 Good Counsel Drive, P.O. Box 669, Mankato, Minnesota 56002.
www.capstonepress.com

1 2 3 4 5 6 13 12 11 10 09 08

Library of Congress Cataloging-in-Publication Data
Schaefer, Lola M., 1950–
    Fathers/by Lola M. Schaefer. — Rev. and updated.
    p. cm. — (Pebble books. Families)
    Includes bibliographical references and index.
    Summary: "Simple text and photographs present fathers and how they interact
with their families" — Provided by publisher.
    ISBN-13: 978-1-4296-1224-1 (hardcover)
    ISBN-10: 1-4296-1224-X (hardcover)
    ISBN-13: 978-1-4296-1753-6 (softcover)
    ISBN-10: 1-4296-1753-5 (softcover)
    1. Fathers — Juvenile literature. 2. Father and child — Juvenile literature.
I. Title. II. Series.
HQ756.S32 2008
306.874'2 — dc22   2007027092

Note to Parents and Teachers

The Families set supports national social studies standards related
to identifying family members and their roles in the family. This
book describes and illustrates fathers. The images support early
readers in understanding the text. The repetition of words and
phrases helps early readers learn new words. This book also
introduces early readers to subject-specific vocabulary words, which
are defined in the glossary section. Early readers may need some
assistance to read some words and to use the Table of Contents,
Glossary, Read More, Internet Sites, and Index sections of the book.

Table of Contents

Fathers

A father is a male parent.
Fathers have children.

mother

sister

father

brothers

5

6

At Home

Libby's dad
makes her a snack.

Bob's dad
does the laundry.

Sal's dad tucks him
into bed.

Work and Play

Ashley's dad goes shopping.

Ben's dad fixes cars.

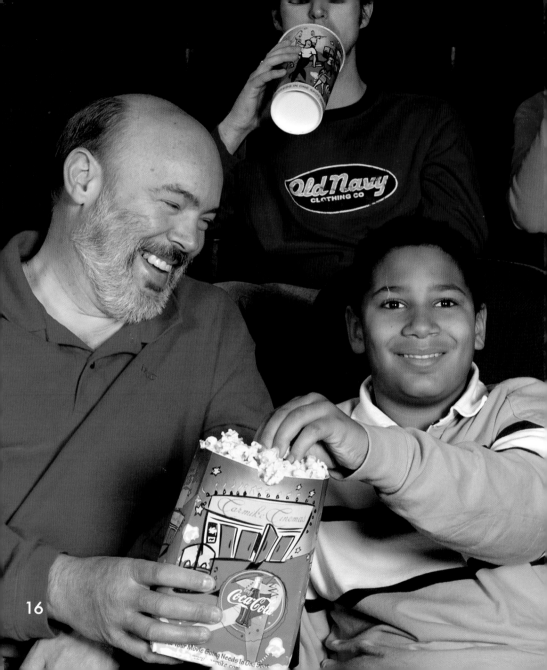

Frank's dad takes him
to the movies.

Kelsey's dad reads.

Fathers love.

Glossary

laundry — clothes, towels, sheets and other items that are being washed or that are clean from washing and drying

parent — a mother or a father of one child or many children; when a parent has more than one child, the children are called siblings.

snack — a small, light meal

tuck — to put to bed and cover snugly

Read More

Kerley, Barbara. *You and Me Together: Moms, Dads, and Kids around the World.* Washington, D.C.: National Geographic, 2005.

Kuklin, Susan. *Families.* New York: Hyperion Books for Children, 2006.

Internet Sites

FactHound offers a safe, fun way to find Internet sites related to this book. All of the sites on FactHound have been researched by our staff.

Here's how:

1. Visit *www.facthound.com*
2. Choose your grade level.
3. Type in this book ID **142961224X** for age-appropriate sites. You may also browse subjects by clicking on letters, or by clicking on pictures and words.
4. Click on the **Fetch It** button.

FactHound will fetch the best sites for you!

Index

Word Count: 46
Grade 1
Early-Intervention Level: 10

Editorial Credits
Sarah L. Schuette, revised edition editor; Kim Brown, revised edition designer

Photo Credits
Capstone Press/Karon Dubke, all